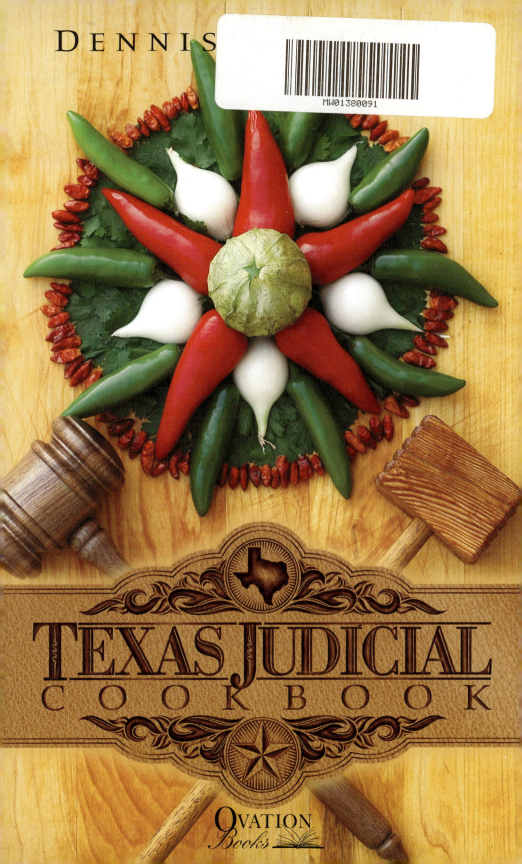

Texas Judicial Cookbook

Published by Ovation Books
P.O. Box 80107
Austin, TX 78758

Produced in association with Mott Publications.

For more information about our books, please write to us, call 512.478.2028, or visit our website at www.ovationbooks.net.

Printed and bound in China. All rights reserved. No part of this book may be reproduced in any form or by any electronic or mechanical means including information storage and retrieval systems without permission in writing from the copyright holder, except by a reviewer, who may quote brief passages in review.

Distributed to the trade by National Book Network, Inc.

Library of Congress Cataloging-in-Publication available upon request.

ISBN-13: 978-0-9790275-2-9
ISBN-10: 0-9790275-2-7

Copyright© 2007 by Dennis R. Mott

The office status of various county officials is representative of their positions held at the time of publication.

10 9 8 7 6 5 4 3 2 1

Introduction

In 1999 former Governor George W. Bush and the Texas Legislature established the Historic Courthouse Preservation Program to provide grants to counties in need of courthouse renovations. This was prompted by the addition of Texas's courthouses to the 1998 list of America's 11 Most Endangered Historic Places by the National Trust for Historic Preservation. Texas has more than 230 historic courthouses, a number unmatched by any other state. According to the National Trust, "The historic seats of county government in Texas represent some of the finest works of public architecture in the Lone Star State—and the nation. Their location and design helped establish each county's unique identity while embodying the majesty, solidity and egalitarian ideals of democratic government."

The Texas Judicial Cookbook is a culinary tribute to these monuments of justice and leadership, fashioned by the hands of pioneering Texans. This compilation of recipes from residing judges, former judges and other state and county officials is enhanced by beautiful photographs of these historical treasures.

Table of Contents

Introduction iii

McLennan County 1
    Jim Lewis Casserole 3

Hopkins County 5
    Hopkins County Stew 7

Hill County 9
    Cheese Dip 11

Ellis County 13
    Gobs 15

Freestone County 17
    Cornbread Salad 19

Bell County 21
    Taco Soup 23
    Marinated Vegetables 24

Gonzales County 25
    Mountain Oysters 27

Robertson County 29
    Rotel 31

Mitchell County 33
    Cowboy Chow 35

Erath County 37
    Fruit Filled Tortillas 39

Bandera County 41
    Evans' Spicy Sausage 43

Harris County 45
    Black Bean Salsa 47
    Corn Casserole 48
    Fruit Dip 49
    Grandma Jasso's Salsa 50

Texas Judicial Cookbook

Hummingbird Cake 51
Chicken Breast Florentine 53
Quick Italian Cream Cake 55

LAVACA COUNTY 57
Blueberry Streusel Coffee Cake 59
Randy's Favorite Chicken Spaghetti Soup 61

MASON COUNTY 63
Banana Bread 65

SHACKELFORD COUNTY 67
7 Rib Prime Rib 69

TOM GREEN COUNTY 71
Swick's Love Muffins 73

JEFFERSON COUNTY 75
Braised Doves 77
Chicken Pork Jambalaya 78
Italian Batter-Fried Shark Bites 79
Quailgerson 80
Judge Layne Walker's Bean Dip 81
Crawfish and Rice 82
Judge Ronald L. Walker's Pretzel Salad 83
Jailhouse Rolls 85

UVALDE COUNTY 87
Katie's Cranberry Chicken 89

VICTORIA COUNTY 91
Pimento Cheese 93

GRIMES COUNTY 95
Red Lobster Biscuits 97

BEXAR COUNTY 99
Snowballs 101

FAYETTE COUNTY 103
Cream Cheese and Poppy Seed Kolache Rolls 105

TABLE OF CONTENTS

Table of Contents

LEE COUNTY 107
    Chicken 'N Rice 109
CONCHO COUNTY 111
    Lasagna 113
JASPER COUNTY 115
    Hot Fried Cornbread 117
    Broccoli Salad 118
    Old Fashioned Southern Pecan Pie 119
THROCKMORTON COUNTY 121
    Company Rice 123
    Ruth's Salad 124
GLASSCOCK COUNTY 125
    Apple Dumplings 127
WILSON COUNTY 129
    Alene's Salad 131
    Fresh Apple Cake 132

OTHER OFFICIALS
BARBARA BUSH
    All-American Clam Chowder 133
LAURA BUSH
    Carrot Muffins 134
RICK PERRY
    Chuck Wagon Chili 135
    Aunt Gene's Coconut Pie 137
JANET STAPLES
    Mom's Chicken Pot Pie 139
MIKE HAMILTON
    Philadelphia Creamy Salsa Dip 140

TEXAS JUDICIAL COOKBOOK

Texas Judicial Cookbook

George Bush
President Bush's Favorite Brownies 141

George W. Bush
President Bush's Favorite Crab Cakes 143

Tom Craddick
Rum Cake 145

Leticia Van de Putte
Taco Pie 147

Kay Bailey Hutchison
Cousin Susie's Perfect Fudge 149
Easy, Hearty Corn Chowder 150

Citations 151

Table of Contents

McLennan County

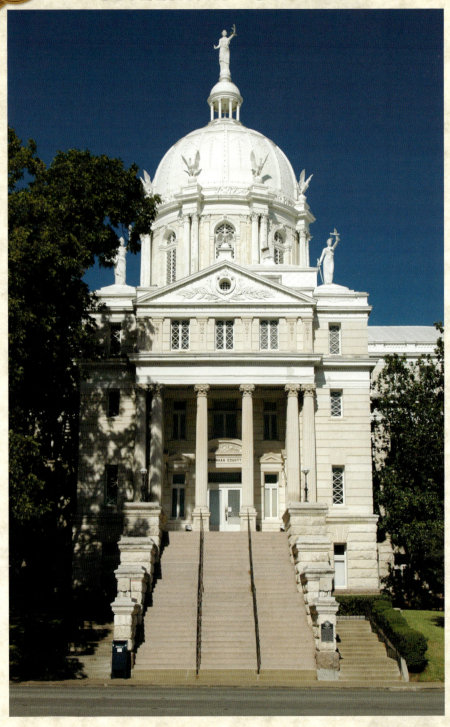

Waco, Texas

McLennan County

Jim Lewis Casserole

*Submitted by Jim Lewis,
McLennan County Judge*

Ingredients:

1 bag (2 lb.) frozen hash brown potatoes, thawed
1 cup sour cream
1 can undiluted cream of chicken soup
½ cup melted butter
½ cup chopped onion
1 teaspoon salt
2 cups grated cheese
½ teaspoon pepper

Texas Judicial Cookbook

Preparation:

- Mix ingredients and place in 13 x 9 inch casserole dish.
- Cook at 350° for 45 to 60 minutes.
- Casserole may be topped with crushed corn flakes before baking or 1 can of onion rings after baking.

NOTE: *Chopped ham may also be added to make a main dish.*

Beaux-Arts design by James Riely Gordon Date – 1901

On January 22, 1850, McLennan County was established by the Texas legislature. It was named for Neil McLennan, one of its early settlers.

During the Reconstruction period, the district judge and the county commissioners of McLennan County arrested each other. The judge charged the commissioners with contempt and the commissioners charged the judge with lunacy. Eventually, cooler heads prevailed and the charges were dropped.

Waco, Texas

Hopkins County

Sulphur Springs, Texas

Hopkins County

Hopkins County Stew

Submitted by Cletis Millsap, Hopkins County Judge

Ingredients:

2 lbs. skinless chicken pieces (or beef)
4 cups water
1½ teaspoon salt
4 medium potatoes diced
1 large onion
1 15 oz. can tomato sauce
1 14½ oz. can peeled, diced tomatoes
1 teaspoon salt
1 teaspoon pepper
1 teaspoon chili powder
1 teaspoon paprika
1 16 oz. can whole kernel corn
1 16 oz. can cream style corn

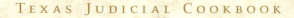

Texas Judicial Cookbook

Preparation:

- Divide first three ingredients in a 5 quart sauce pan until chicken is tender. Reserving liquid, remove chicken pieces to be cooled, deboned and diced.

- Add to liquid, potatoes and onions. If needed, add enough water to JUST COVER these veggies and cook until potatoes are done.

- Add diced chicken, pepper, tomato sauce, diced tomatoes, salt, chili powder and paprika. Bring to a boil.

- Add whole kernel and cream style corn while stirring to prevent scorching.

- Reduce heat to simmer. If needed, add water to fill pot. Cover and simmer for 15 minutes, stirring as needed.

- Serve with crackers or cornbread, cheese and pickles.

NOTE: *This recipe is a basic stew recipe and other ingredients may be added to suit individual taste.*

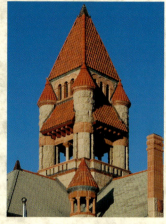

Romanesque Revival design by James Riely Gordon Date – 1895

Before the courthouse was complete, a petition was circulated asking for a clock to be placed in the tower. County officials decided that the placing of a clock in the spire would be allowed only if it could be done with no cost to the county. It was discussed among interested citizens but no action was taken. The commissioner at the time, R. Carpenter, said of the proposal, "Get up at sunup, go to bed at dark, and eat when you are hungry, and you don't need no d--- clock."

Sulphur Springs, Texas

Hill County

Hillsboro, Texas

Hill County

Cheese Dip

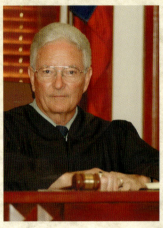

*Submitted by Kenneth Davis,
Hill County Judge*

Ingredients:

1 pound (small box) Velveeta Cheese
1 can original Rotel tomatoes
1 can cream of mushroom soup
½ pound hamburger meat, cooked

Texas Judicial Cookbook

Texas Judicial Cookbook

Preparation:

- Melt Velveeta and Rotel together in microwave.
- Add 1 can Cream of Mushroom soup and ½ pound cooked hamburger meat.
- Microwave again until bubbly.
- Serve with Doritos.

NOTE: *If you like, you can cook chopped onion with meat.*

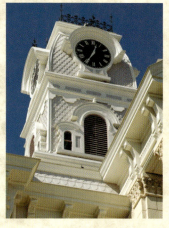

Designed by W. C. Dodson
Date – 1890

Hill County was named for Dr. George Washington Hill, who had served as President Sam Houston's Secretary of War.

The county seat was originally called Hillsborough, but the town's name was changed to Hillsboro in 1854 when the Post Office changed all names ending in "borough" to "boro."

Helpful Hint: If any food splatters in the microwave and is hard to clean up, simply boil a mixture of 1 cup of water and 1/4 cup of vinegar in the microwave. This deodorizes and loosens the mess for a much easier cleanup.

Hillsboro, Texas

Ellis County

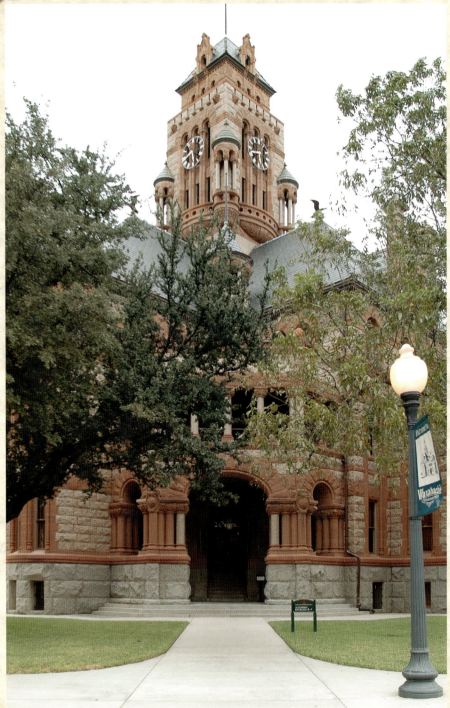

Waxahachie, Texas

Ellis County

Gobs

*Submitted by Chad Adams,
Ellis County Judge*

Ingredients:

COOKIES:

2 cups sugar

½ cup Crisco

2 eggs

4 cups flour (all-purpose)

2 teaspoons soda

½ teaspoon baking powder

½ cup cocoa

1 cup sour milk, or 1 cup sweet milk plus 1 tablespoon vinegar

1 teaspoon vanilla

1 cup boiling water

FILLING:

5 tablespoons flour

1 cup milk

1 cup Crisco

¾ cup confectioner's sugar

½ teaspoon salt

Texas Judicial Cookbook

Preparation:

COOKIES:

- Cream together sugar, Crisco and eggs.
- Sift together flour, soda, baking powder and cocoa. Add to creamed mixture.
- Add milk and vanilla.
- At very last, add boiling water.
- Chill batter in refrigerator while making the filling.
- Take batter, drop like cookies and bake for about 7 minutes at 400°-425°F.
- When cookies are cool, spread with filling and put together so as to make a sandwich.

FILLING:

- Cream together Crisco, confectioner's sugar and salt.
- Cook milk and flour to thick paste, cool. Drop by spoonfuls into creamed mix.

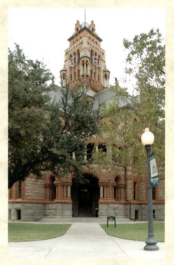

*Romanesque Revival Style
by James Riely Gordon
Date – 1897*

Construction of the Ellis County courthouse was steeped in controversy and litigation from the outset. The need, cost and site location were matter of heated debate. One county commissioner refused to appear at meetings to raise taxes in order to fund the project and was therefore removed from office by the district judge. After months of squabbling, the cornerstone was eventually laid on July 4, 1895.

Waxahachie, Texas

Freestone County

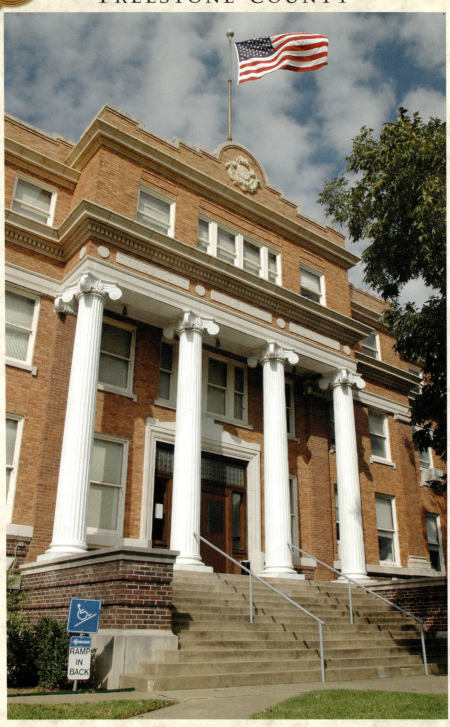

Fairfield, Texas

Freestone County

Cornbread Salad

*Submitted by
Sheriff Ralph Billings,
Freestone County*

Ingredients:

3 family-size pans of cornbread, baked and crumbled

4 chopped onions

4 bell pepper, chopped

4 large tomatoes, chopped

6-8 stalks celery, chopped

4 cans whole-kernel corn, drained

2-3 jars pimientos, drained

3-4 cups mayonnaise or salad dressing, Miracle Whip

Texas Judicial Cookbook

PREPARATION:

- Mix ingredients, chill, and serve.

NOTE: *Serves 40 people.*

*Classical Revival design
by W.R. Kaufman
Date – 1919*

Blues musician, Blind Lemon Jefferson, was born in Coutchman, Texas (Northern Freestone County), in July of 1897. Born blind, Jefferson is recognized as one of the earliest representatives of the "classic blues" field and was inducted into the Blues Foundation's Hall of Fame in 1980.

Helpful Hint: To lower the fat content of your cornbread, use cream style corn instead of oil.

Fairfield, Texas

Bell County

Belton, Texas

Bell County

Taco Soup

Submitted by Martha J. Trudo, 264th District Judge, Bell County

Ingredients:

1 or 1½ lbs hamburger meat
1 medium onion
1 large can crushed tomatoes
1 can Rotel tomatoes (Hot, if you like)
1 envelope taco seasoning
1 envelope Ranch dressing
2 cans whole yellow corn with liquid
2 cans kidney beans with liquid

Preparation:

- Brown hamburger and onions together, then drain the fat.
- Add remaining ingredients.
- Add water and cook to suit your taste and eat.

Texas Judicial Cookbook

Marinated Vegetables

Ingredients:

1 can shoepeg corn
1 can French style green beans
1 can kidney beans
1 can English peas
2 oz jar of pimentos
½ cup chopped onion
½ cup chopped celery
½ cup chopped green pepper
¾ cup white vinegar
½ cup vegetable oil
1 cup sugar
½ teaspoon pepper

Preparation:

- Mix together first 8 ingredients, drain and set aside.
- Combine vinegar, vegetable oil, sugar, and pepper, boil until sugar is dissolved. Let cool, pour over the drained vegetables.
- Let sit in refrigerator overnight and serve.

Renaissance Revival design by Jasper N. Preston and Sons
Date – 1884

Bell County, named for Peter H. Bell, was formed on January 22, 1850.

The Bird's Creek Indian Fight of May 26, 1839, a bloody brawl between Texas Rangers and Comanche Indians, took place about one and a half miles northwest of present-day Temple.

Belton, Texas

Gonzales County

Gonzales, Texas

Gonzales County

Mountain Oysters

*Submitted by David Bird,
Gonzales County Judge*

Ingredients:

25 lbs. Mountain Oysters
Commercial frying oil or lard
Couple bags of cornmeal
Salt and Pepper
Ketchup
Tabasco

SKINNING PARTY:

The evening before Oysters are to be fried a skinning party is held. Frozen mountain oysters should be thawed approximately 1 hour so that the skin is thawed but inside is still frozen. Four people can skin and cut up oysters fairly quickly if they have one person with clean hands maintaining their refreshments.

Texas Judicial Cookbook

Texas Judicial Cookbook

Preparation:

Oysters need to be cut into ½" x ¾" – 1" x 1½" – 2" long pieces for optimum frying size. This is very easy if they have not fully thawed. Once cut up place in large bowls, small buckets or turned over cake covers. Refrigerate until time to cook next day.

DEEP FRYING:

Commercial frying oil is easiest to use when cooking as it doesn't burn as bad as lard. Of course, it doesn't taste as good either. A regular fish frying pot and basket are a good size to use. Pick up a couple bags of cornmeal, salt and pepper, ketchup, Tabasco and several beer flats. Mix cornmeal and salt and pepper to taste in beer flat. Put two handfuls of oysters into the cornmeal mixture. Shake and drop in basket. Fry like fish. Eat plain or with ketchup and Tabasco. Fittin' to eat either way.

NOTE: *For a Good-sized party of 50 or Hors d'oeuvres for more.*

*Designed by James Riely Gordon
Date – 1896*

Clock tower legend: In 1921, Albert Howard awaited his death within sight of Gonzales's clock tower. He cursed the clocks he stared at as he counted down his time to live and swore that they would prove his innocence. After he was hanged the four clocks never told the same time.

Gonzales, Texas

Robertson County

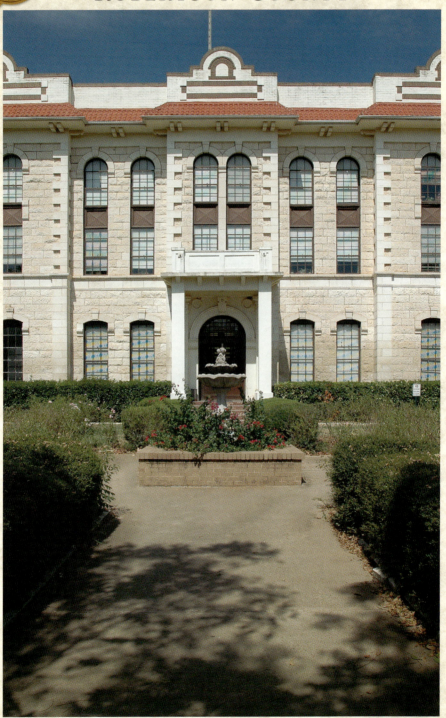

Franklin, Texas

Robertson County

Rotel

Ingredients:

1 lb. browned ground meat
1 can mushroom soup
1 can Rotel tomatoes & green chiles
1 cup water
2 cups cooked elbow macaroni

Submitted by Fred Elliot, Robertson County Judge, and wife, Judy

Texas Judicial Cookbook

TEXAS JUDICIAL COOKBOOK

PREPARATION:

- Drain meat, add mushroom soup, water, Rotel tomatoes and macaroni.
- Let simmer for about 30 minutes. Stir as needed

NOTE: *Our family likes this served with salad and hot rolls.*

*Second Empire design by F. E. Ruffini
Date – 1882*

On December 14, 1837, the First Texas Congress established Robertson County and named it in honor of Sterling Robertson.

Robertson County has had five County Seats: Old Franklin, Wheelock, Owensville, Calvert and Franklin.

Food Fact: RO*TEL began in the early 1940s when Carl Roettele opened a small canning plant in Elsa, Texas.

FRANKLIN, TEXAS

Mitchell County

Colorado City, Texas

MITCHELL COUNTY

Cowboy Chow

INGREDIENTS:

1 14 oz. package smoked sausage, cut into bite-size pieces

1 cup thick and chunky salsa

1 cup original barbecue sauce

1 10 oz. can whole kernel corn, drained

1 15½ oz. can dark red kidney beans, drained

1 53 oz. can pork and beans, drained

½ cup chopped onion

*Submitted by Ray Mayo,
Mitchell County Judge*

Texas Judicial Cookbook

Texas Judicial Cookbook

Preparation:

- Spray a large saucepan with nonfat cooking spray. In the saucepan combine the sausage, salsa, barbecue sauce, corn, kidney beans, pork and beans and onion until well mixed.

- Bring to a boil. Reduce heat to low. Cover and simmer for 5 minutes.

- Serve with cornbread and sliced jalepeños on the side.

Classical Revival design by David Castle
Date – 1924

Due to a surveyor's mistake, the 1883 courthouse was built in Oak Street instead of facing Oak Street. To fix this the building was simply demolished and started over in the correct location.

Helpful Hint: To cut through tough grease on dishes, add a tablespoon of vinegar to your hot, soapy dishwater.

Colorado City, Texas

Erath County

Stephenville, Texas

Erath County

Fruit Filled Tortillas

Submitted by Bart McDougal, County Court at Law Judge, Erath County

Ingredients:

2 cans fruit pie filling of choice – Peach, Apple, Cherry, Apricot, Strawberry, Blueberry

1 12 count package of flour tortillas (medium size)

1½ cups sugar

2½ sticks butter (not margarine)

1 cup water

½ cup chopped pecans

1 to 2 teaspoons cinnamon, according to preference

Texas Judicial Cookbook

Preparation:

- Place 6 tortillas at a time on wax or parchment paper.
- Open one can of the pie filling and distribute the fruit evenly down the middle of each tortilla, using the entire can of fruit.
- Roll up tortilla tightly and place in 9 x 13 inch dish sprayed with Pam.
- Repeat with the other 6 tortillas and other can of pie filling. They will be close together in the dish. Set aside.
- In a saucepan, heat the sugar, butter, and water until sugar melts then boil for 3 minutes. Watch it carefully so it does not boil over.
- When heated, pour mixture over all of the tortillas.
- Let it set, lightly covered, for one hour.
- When ready to cook, sprinkle the cinnamon and nuts over the top.
- Bake in a 350° degree oven for one hour.

Designed by James Riely Gordon
Date – 1892

The county was named for George B. Erath, who fought in the Texas Revolution, including the Battle of San Jacinto.

Stephenville, Texas

Bandera County

Bandera, Texas

BANDERA COUNTY

Evans' Spicy Sausage

Submitted by Richard Evans,
Bandera County Judge

INGREDIENTS:

5 lbs. ground meat
(lean beef, deer or wild hog)

¼ cup meat cure mix (Morton brand)

2½ tablespoons coarse ground black pepper

1 tablespoon crushed red pepper

2½ teaspoons mustard seed

1½ teaspoons garlic powder

2½ tablespoons liquid smoke

Texas Judicial Cookbook

Preparation:

- Combine all ingredients; mix well; chill 8 hours.
- Shape mixture into 5 logs.
- Wrap logs in cheesecloth; tie ends with string.
- Place on rack in shallow pan and bake for 6 hours at 200°.
- Chill overnight before serving.

Renaissance Revival design by B. F. Trester
Date - 1890

The county name was derived from the Spanish word for "flag."

Food Fact: Venison is one of the lowest fat, lowest cholesterol meats you can eat. To help avoid the wild taste, soak it in lightly salted water overnight.

Bandera, Texas

Harris County

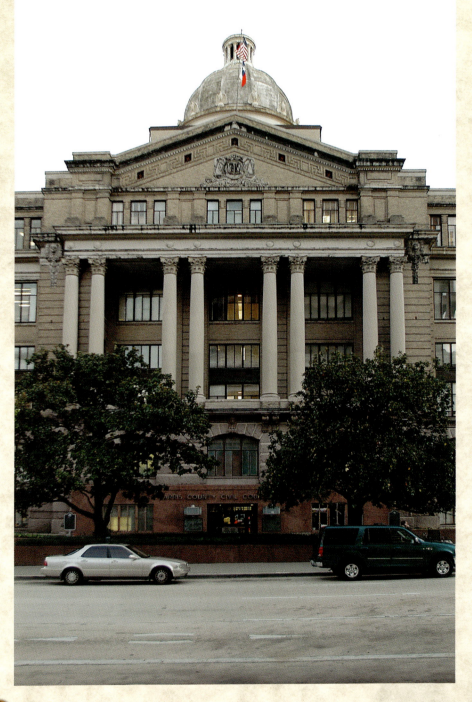

HOUSTON, TEXAS

Harris County

Black Bean Salsa

*Submitted by Tommy Thomas,
Harris County Sheriff*

Ingredients:

1 can black beans – drained and rinsed
1 can corn – drained
½ small red onion – chopped
1 bunch cilantro – chopped
Juice from 3 squeezed limes
1 teaspoon cumin
½ teaspoon chili powder
Salt and pepper to taste
Chopped tomato (optional)

Preparation:

- Mix and serve with chips or as a salad

Texas Judicial Cookbook

Texas Judicial Cookbook

Corn Casserole

Ingredients:

1 box Jiffy corn mix
1 cup sour cream
1 can whole kernel corn (drained)
1 can cream corn
1 stick margarine (melted)
Salt & pepper
Shredded cheddar cheese (to top casserole)

*Submitted by
Candy S. Henderson,
Major,
Harris County Sheriff's Office*

Preparation:

- Mix all together-pour batter into 9 x 11 inch buttered baking dish, put shredded cheddar cheese on top.

- Bake at 350° for 30 minutes.

NOTE: *Serve as a plea bargain bread.*

Houston, Texas

Harris County

Fruit Dip

*Submitted by
Patricia Ann Diaz,
Harris County Sheriff's Office*

Ingredients:

1 8 oz. package cream cheese

1 cup powdered sugar

1 teaspoon vanilla

8 oz. Cool Whip

Preparation:

- Mix cream cheese and powdered sugar. Add vanilla and Cool Whip. Chill.

NOTE: *Serve with fruit.*

Texas Judicial Cookbook

Texas Judicial Cookbook

Grandma Jasso's Salsa

Ingredients:

5-6 fresh jalapeños
¼ teaspoon garlic powder
¼ teaspoon salt
¼ cup water
1 medium tomato

Preparation:

- Boil jalapeños and tomato until soft. Drain water.
- Place jalapeños and tomato in a blender; add water, garlic powder, and salt.

Submitted by Ruben Diaz, Lieutenant, Harris County Sheriff's Office

Houston, Texas

Harris County

Hummingbird Cake

*Submitted by
Tamara Dubrevil,
Administrative Assistant,
Harris County Sheriff's Office*

Ingredients:

3 cups all-purpose flour, sifted before measuring

2 cups sugar

1 teaspoon salt

1 teaspoon baking soda

1 teaspoon ground cinnamon

3 eggs, beaten

1½ cups vegetable oil

1½ teaspoon vanilla

1 8 oz. can crushed pineapples

2 cups chopped pecans, divided

1½ cups chopped bananas

CREAM CHEESE FROSTING:

1 8 oz. pkg. of cream cheese, softened to room temperature

½ cup butter or margarine, softened

2 cups (or one 16-oz. box) powdered sugar

1 teaspoon vanilla

1 cup coconut

1 cup remaining chopped pecans

PREPARATION:

CAKE:

- Combine flour, sugar, salt, soda, and cinnamon in a large mixing bowl. Add eggs and oil. Stir until dry ingredients are moistened. Do not beat. Stir in vanilla, pineapple, 1 cup of nuts and 1 cup of bananas. Mix well. Spoon batter into 3 well-greased and floured 9-inch pans. You can also use non-stick cooking spray.

- Bake 30-40 minutes at 350°. Cool in pans for 10 minutes. Remove from pans and cool completely before icing.

FROSTING:

- Combine cream cheese and butter. Cream until smooth. Add powdered sugar; beat until fluffy. Stir in vanilla. Spread between the layers and on top and sides of cake. Sprinkle with remaining 1 cup chopped nuts and coconut between layers. Sprinkle nuts on top.

NOTE: *Bananas may be chopped in blender.*

*Beaux-Arts style
by Lang, Winchell & Barglebaugh
Date – 1910*

On December 22, 1836, the First Congress formed Harrisburg County. In 1839 the name was changed to Harris County, in honor of John R. Harris.

HOUSTON, TEXAS

Harris County

Chicken Breast Florentine

*Submitted by Linda Green,
Crime Analyst,
Harris County Sheriff's Office*

Ingredients:

1 10-oz. bag spinach, rinsed
1 clove garlic, minced
Ground pepper to taste
2 oz. cooked lean ham, cut into strips
¼ teaspoon dried thyme
4 chicken breasts, skinless and boneless
4 teaspoon olive oil
½ cup dry white wine
¼ teaspoon salt

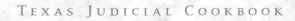

TEXAS JUDICIAL COOKBOOK

Preparation:

- Heat large skillet; add spinach, garlic, and pepper. Cook covered until spinach wilts, about 2 minutes.
- Let cool, squeeze out excess liquid, stir in ham and a pinch of thyme.
- Cut a long, thin pocket into each chicken breast; stuff spinach mixture into pockets.
- Seal closed with toothpicks.
- In same skillet, heat oil; add chicken, brown on each side.
- Add wine, salt, and remaining thyme.
- Simmer covered until chicken is cooked, about 10 minutes.
- Served topped with pan juices.

NOTES: *Serves 4, 181 calories, 6 grams fat, and 1 gram fiber.*

Harris County's first courthouse was built in 1883 by Edward J. Duhamel. Due to overcrowding it was demolished after twenty-four years. The next courthouse, by Lang & Witchell, was completed in 1910 but was not formally dedicated until March 2, 1911, Texas's seventy-fifth anniversary of independence and the 180th anniversary of Sam Houston's birth.

Houston, Texas

Harris County

Quick Italian Cream Cake

Submitted by Beverly Falcon, Deputy, Harris County Sheriff's Office

Ingredients:

1 package white cake mix with pudding
3 eggs
1¼ cups buttermilk
¼ cup vegetable oil
1 can flake coconut
⅔ cup chopped pecans

CREAM CHEESE FROSTING:
1 8 oz. package cream cheese, softened
½ cup butter, softened
1 box powdered sugar
2 teaspoon vanilla
1 cup chopped pecans
Coconut, if desired

TEXAS JUDICIAL COOKBOOK

Preparation:

CAKE:

- Beat first 4 ingredients for 2 minutes at medium speed.
- Stir in coconut and pecans.
- Pour into 3 greased and floured 9-inch round cake pans or a 9 x 13 inch baking pan.
- Bake at 350° for 20-30 minutes until cake tests done. Cool and frost.

CREAM CHEESE FROSTING:

- Beat together cream cheese, butter, and vanilla until smooth.
- Add powdered sugar and beat until light and fluffy.
- Stir in pecans and coconut. Frost cake.

NOTE: *Simply delicious.*

Since its first log courthouse, Harris County has built four successive structures on the courthouse square in Houston.

Houston, Texas

Lavaca County

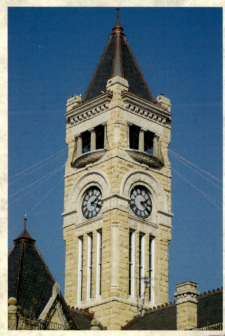

Hallettsville, Texas

Lavaca County

Blueberry Streusel Coffee Cake

Submitted by Ronald Leck, Lavaca County Judge, and wife, Mary

Ingredients:

2 cups all-purpose flour
¾ cup sugar
2 teaspoons baking powder
¼ teaspoon salt
1 egg
½ cup milk
½ cup butter, softened
1 cup fresh or frozen blueberries
1 cup chopped pecans

Streusel Topping:

½ cup sugar
⅓ cup all-purpose flour
¼ cup cold butter

Texas Judicial Cookbook

Preparation:

- In a large mixing bowl, combine the flour, sugar, baking powder and salt.
- Add egg, milk and butter; beat well.
- Fold in blueberries and pecans.
- Spread into a greased 9 inch square baking pan.
- For topping, combine sugar and flour in a bowl; cut in butter until crumbly.
- Sprinkle over batter.
- Bake at 375° for 35-40 minutes or until a toothpick inserted near the center comes out clean. Cool on a wire rack.

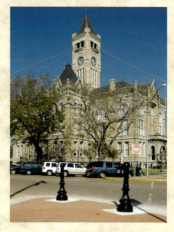

Designed by Eugene Heiner
Date – 1897

Since La Grange declined the honor of having the film version of The Best Little Whorehouse in Texas *filmed there, the people of Hallettsville volunteered their town for the courthouse sequences.*

Hallettsville, Texas

Lavaca County

Randy's Favorite Chicken Spaghetti Soup

Ingredients:

3-4 chicken leg quarters
1 large bell pepper
1 large onion
1 8 oz. can of mushroom stems and pieces
1 can diced tomatoes
1 4 oz. can tomato sauce
1 16 oz. bag wide egg noodles

*Submitted by Randy Schlauch,
Hallettsville Chief of Police,
Lavaca County*

Texas Judicial Cookbook

Preparation:

- Boil leg quarters in large pot of salted water for 45 minutes.
- While it is boiling, dice the pepper and onion. Remove chicken onto a plate to cool.
- Sauté onion and pepper in butter until clear and soft. Add mushrooms, juice and all. Pour this vegetable mixture into the chicken broth. Add tomatoes and sauce.
- Cut up chicken into small pieces and add to the pot along with egg noodles.
- Simmer 15-20 minutes or until noodles are done.

Enjoy!

Lavaca's courthouse tower is two stories tall and contains a seven-foot Seth Thomas clock.

Hallettsville, Texas

Mason County

Mason, Texas

Mason County

Banana Bread

Submitted by Jerry Bearden, Mason County Judge

Ingredients:

2½ cups flour

2 cups sugar

½ teaspoon salt

¾ cup oil

3 eggs

1 teaspoon vanilla

1⅓ teaspoon baking soda

¼ cup buttermilk

1 cup chopped nuts

4 large bananas, slightly mashed

Texas Judicial Cookbook

TEXAS JUDICIAL COOKBOOK

Preparation:

- Bake 1 hour at 350°.

NOTE: *Makes 5 small or 2 large loaves.*

Classical Revival design by E. H. Hosford & Co. Date – 1909

The Mason County War lasted from 1875 to 1877. It began as a feud over cattle rustling (the stealing and killing of cattle) but, after many fatalities, grew into a racial conflict between Germans and Americans.

Food Fact: Freezing overripe bananas before you are ready to use them will release even more flavor in your banana bread.

Mason, Texas

SHACKELFORD COUNTY

Albany, Texas

SHACKELFORD COUNTY

7 Rib Prime Rib

*Submitted by Ross Montgomery,
Shackelford County Judge*

INGREDIENTS:

Prime Rib
Salt
Pepper
Paprika
Parsley

Texas Judicial Cookbook

Preparation:

- White with salt.
- Black with pepper.
- Red with paprika.
- Green with parsley.
- Cook at 325°
  15 minutes per pound for rare
  19 minutes per pound for medium

Second Empire design
by J. E. Flanders
Date – 1883

In order to attend jury duty or deal with other legal matters, many citizens from the Shackelford area had to make the long trek to the court of far-off Jack County. In 1874 they petitioned to organize a new county. It was named in honor of Dr. Jack Shackelford, a Texas revolutionary hero.

Helpful Hint: To cook your meat well done, it should reach a temperature of 160° to 170° Fahrenheit. For medium well, which is slightly pinker, it should reach 150° to 155°. Remember that cutting meat to check how well it is done will dry it out quicker.

Albany, Texas

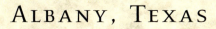

Tom Green County

San Angelo, Texas

Tom Green County

Swick's Love Muffins

Submitted by Randy Swick, Tom Green County DPS

Ingredients:

2 cups all-purpose flour
1 egg
⅓ cup vegetable oil
¾ cup milk
½ teaspoon salt
¼ cup firmly packed brown sugar
¼ cup granulated sugar
2 teaspoons baking powder
½ cup baking soda
2 cups chocolate chips
½ cup chopped maraschino cherries

Texas Judicial Cookbook

Preparation:

- In a large bowl, combine 1¾ cups chocolate chips, brown sugar, granulated sugar, baking powder, baking soda, and salt.
- In a separate bowl, mix milk, oil, and egg until blended.
- Add milk mixture to dry ingredients just until moist.
- Divide between 12 paper-and-foil-lined cups.
- Top with remaining chocolate chips.
- Bake in preheated oven on 375° for 18-20 minutes, or until golden brown.
- Cool for 5 minutes.

NOTE: *Best served when warm.*

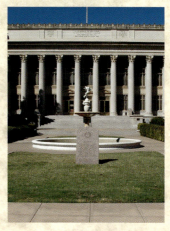

*Classical Revival design
by Anton F. Korn
Date – 1928*

San Angelo, Texas

Jefferson County

Beaumont, Texas

JEFFERSON COUNTY

Braised Doves

*Submitted by Al Gerson,
County Court at Law Judge,
Jefferson County*

INGREDIENTS:

24 doves
¼ cup salt
2 tablespoons red pepper
2 tablespoons chopped bell pepper
¼ cup vinegar or wine
2 tablespoons onion tops
¼ cup oil
¾ cup chopped onions
2 tablespoons chopped bell pepper
2 tablespoons chopped parsley
¼ cup olive oil

PREPARATION:

- Marinate doves with bell pepper, red pepper, and vinegar.
- Brown doves in warm pot; keep seasoning.
- Brown the pepper and onions with all the other ingredients.
- Add ¼ cup of remaining juices and add water for gravy.
- Cook doves in covered pot for 3½ hours.

NOTE: *Serve with wild rice and a bottle of Piney Woods Country Wine.*

TEXAS JUDICIAL COOKBOOK

TEXAS JUDICIAL COOKBOOK

Chicken Pork Jambalaya

Ingredients:

½ lb. pork sausage, fresh
2 cups diced chicken, cooked
1 cup green peppers, chopped
1 cup green onions, chopped
1½ cups water
1 cup rice
1 clove garlic, minced
1½ teaspoons salt
¼ teaspoon thyme
¼ teaspoon Tabasco sauce

*Modern design
by Fred C. Stone & A. Babin
Date – 1931*

Jefferson County was formed in 1836 and was one of the original counties in the Republic of Texas. It was named for Thomas Jefferson.

Preparation:

- Spread pork over bottom of large skillet. Cook 5 minutes; add chicken and cook until brown. Remove from pan.
- Add green pepper, onions, and garlic to some of pork grease and cook until tender.
- Add remaining ingredients. Place chicken and pork on top.
- Cook over low heat for 25 minutes.
- Lift rice with fork gently and cook uncovered 5 minutes.

NOTE: *Makes 4-6 servings.*

BEAUMONT, TEXAS

Jefferson County

Italian Batter-Fried Shark Bites

*Submitted by Al Gerson,
County Court at Law Judge,
Jefferson County*

Ingredients:

2 lbs. shark filets or other fish
1 cup flour
1 tablespoon salt
1 teaspoon baking powder
1 tablespoon white vinegar
Oil for frying

Preparation:

- Cut filets into 1-inch chunks.
- Combine flour, salt, and baking powder.
- Slowly add 1 cup of water and vinegar. Mix well.
- Dip fish cubes into batter and drop into hot oil at 425°. Cook 3-4 minutes or until golden brown. Drain on absorbent paper.

NOTE: Serves 6.

TEXAS JUDICIAL COOKBOOK

Quailgerson

Ingredients:

4-8 quail
1 onion, chopped
1 teaspoon butter
1 4 oz. can mushrooms, drained
1 can cream of chicken soup
½ cup dry white wine
Salt and pepper to taste

Preparation:

- Salt and pepper 4-8 quail inside and out.
- Sauté 1 chopped onion in 1 teaspoon butter. Add can of mushrooms.
- Fill cavities of quail with mixture and place in baking pan.
- Combine cream of chicken soup with ½ cup dry white wine.
- Bake at 275° for 3 hours and baste occasionally.

NOTE: *Serve with wild rice and salad.*

Jefferson became the top rice-producing county in Texas in the 1940s when more than 50,000 acres were planted with rice annually yielding thirteen barrels of rice an acre.

BEAUMONT, TEXAS

JEFFERSON COUNTY

Judge Layne Walker's Bean Dip

Submitted by Layne Walker, 252nd District Judge, Jefferson County, Texas

INGREDIENTS:

2 cups cooked pinto beans
1 onion, chopped
2 tablespoons bacon drippings
1/3 cup Kraft sharp cheddar cheese, grated
4 oz. jalapeño peppers, drained, seeded, and chopped
Salt and pepper to taste

PREPARATION:

- Mash beans until smooth, or blend in blender. Set aside.
- Sauté onion in bacon drippings.
- Add beans and remaining ingredients to onion and stir over low heat until cheese melts.

NOTE: *Serve warm with corn chips.*

TEXAS JUDICIAL COOKBOOK

TEXAS JUDICIAL COOKBOOK

Crawfish and Rice

Ingredients:

2 lbs. crawfish tails
1 can beef broth
1½ cups raw rice
1 medium onion and bell pepper
1 stick butter
Salt
Pepper
Garlic powder

Submitted by Carl Griffith, Jefferson County Judge

Preparation:

- Sauté onion and bell pepper in the butter.
- Add crawfish (salt, pepper and little garlic powder to taste), rice and beef broth. Stir.
- Add all ingredients to rice cooker.

NOTE: *Be sure crawfish tails are defrosted completely.*

BEAUMONT, TEXAS

JEFFERSON COUNTY

Judge Ronald L. Walker's Pretzel Salad

Submitted by Ronald Walker, Former Judge, Jefferson County

INGREDIENTS:

1 cup pretzels, crushed

½ stick oleo

1¼ cups sugar

1 8 oz. package cream cheese, softened

1 8 oz. tub Cool Whip

2 tablespoons cornstarch

20 oz. crushed pineapple, drained, reserving liquid

TEXAS JUDICIAL COOKBOOK

PREPARATION:

- Mix pretzels, butter, and ½ cup sugar together and spread into an 8 x 12 inch dish.
- Bake crust 5 minutes at 350°. Let cool.
- Mix cream cheese, Cool Whip, and ½ cup sugar. Spread over first layer.
- Mix cornstarch, ¼ cup sugar, and pineapple juice drained from the can of crushed pineapples.
- Cook on stove over medium heat until thick. Let cool.
- Stir in crushed pineapple.
- Spread over second layer.

NOTES: *Top with Cool Whip. Chill. Serves 15.*

Jefferson County's economy was transformed by the discovery of oil at Spindletop in 1901. Beaumont's population boomed from 9,000 to 20,000. The oil boom helped Jefferson County through the Great Depression. At the Depression's height, there were almost 2,000 wells in the county producing almost 1,000,000 barrels.

BEAUMONT, TEXAS

JEFFERSON COUNTY

Jailhouse Rolls

INGREDIENTS:

1 cup mashed potatoes
2 sticks oleo
3 whole eggs
7 cups flour
1½ teaspoons salt
1 cup sugar
1½ cups lukewarm water
1 package dry yeast

*Submitted by
Louann, Tracey and
Sergeant Danny G. Walker,
Forensic Crime Scene Unit,
S.W.A.T., Jefferson County
Sheriff's Office*

Texas Judicial Cookbook

Texas Judicial Cookbook

Preparation:

- Mix dry yeast in lukewarm water, blend, set aside for later use.
- Mix potatoes, oleo, eggs, salt and sugar; blend into flour.
- Add yeast water blend well, place into greased bowl.
- Cover with cold, damp cloth and place in refrigerator until ready for use.
- Roll out like piecrust, not as thin - cut to desired size.
- Butter tops, let stand for several hours.
- Bake in preheated oven at 450° for 10 minutes.

NOTE: *For a family of four, this recipe will furnish rolls for about three meals.*

Beaumont, Texas

Uvalde County

Uvalde, Texas

Uvalde County

Katie's Cranberry Chicken

Ingredients:

6 Chicken breasts (boneless, raw)
1 Small bottle of Catalina dressing
1 Can whole cranberries
6 Orange slices
Fresh parsley

*Submitted by
William R. Mitchell,
Uvalde County Judge*

Texas Judicial Cookbook

TEXAS JUDICIAL COOKBOOK

PREPARATION:

- Mix cranberries and Catalina dressing. Pour over chicken and bake at 375° for one hour.
- Garnish with oranges and parsley.

NOTE: *Very good and pretty.*

Texas Renaissance design by Henry Phelps
Date – 1927

Uvalde County is named for Spaniard Juan de Ugalde, known for his campaigns against Indians in Texas.

Food Fact: According to the USDA, fresh or ground chicken should only be refrigerated for one to two days. Leftover cooked chicken is safe in the fridge for three to four days.

UVALDE, TEXAS

Victoria County

Victoria, Texas

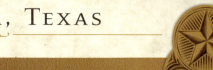

Victoria County

Pimento Cheese

Submitted by Carolyn Milam, Justice of the Peace, Precinct 2, Victoria County

Ingredients:

1 lb. cheddar cheese
1 lb. American cheese
4-5 green onions, chopped
3-4 garlic toes, chopped
4 caps of lemon juice
1 quart Hellman's Mayonnaise
2 oz. sliced or diced pimentos

Texas Judicial Cookbook

Texas Judicial Cookbook

Preparation:

- Grate both kinds of cheese.
- Add remaining ingredients. Use enough mayonnaise for easy spreading.
- Spread on crackers or breads.

NOTES: *Can sprinkle a little garlic powder to taste - if desired.*

Make ahead as it ages well.

Romanesque Revival design by James Riely Gordon
Date – 1892

The city of Victoria is dubbed the "crossroads of South Texas" because of the convergence of roads from Houston, San Antonio, Austin and Corpus Christi.

Victoria was one of the original twenty-three counties established by the First Congress of the Republic of Texas on March 17, 1836.

Victoria, Texas

Grimes County

Anderson, Texas

Grimes County

Red Lobster Biscuits

Ingredients:

2 cups buttermilk baking mix
¼ cup butter or oleo, melted
⅔ cup milk
½ teaspoon garlic powder
½ cup shredded Cheddar cheese

*Submitted by James P. Dixon,
Grimes County Judge*

Texas Judicial Cookbook

Preparation:

- With a wooden spoon, mix together baking mix, milk and cheese until a soft dough forms. Beat vigorously for 30 seconds.

- Drop dough by heaping tablespoonfuls onto an ungreased baking sheet. Bake 8 to 10 minutes at 450° until golden brown.

- Combine melted butter or oleo and garlic powder; brush over warm biscuits before removing from baking sheet. Serve warm.

NOTE: *Makes 10 to 12 biscuits.*

*Italianate design
by F. S. Glover
Date – 1893*

The county was named for Jesse Grimes, a signer of the Texas Declaration of Independence and State Senator.

Helpful Hint: Wrap any leftover bread in foil and store it on a low shelf in the refrigerator. It will keep up to three weeks.

Anderson, Texas

Bexar County

SAN ANTONIO, TEXAS

Bexar County

Snowballs

*Submitted by
Karen Crouch (Flores),
Bexar County Judge,
and family*

In my husband's family: Gusanitos
In my family: Snowballs
In Austria: Kipfel
In Greece: Kourambiethes

Ingredients:

1 cup butter or shortening
¼ cup confectioner's sugar
2 teaspoons vanilla
1 tablespoon water
2 cups flour
½ cup or a little more finely chopped pecans or walnuts

Texas Judicial Cookbook

Preparation:

- Cream butter and sugar.
- Add vanilla, water, flour, and nuts. Mix well!
- Roll into shape-
- - In my husband's family they were made in the shape of a worm
- - In my family they were made in the shape of a ball
- Bake at 325° F for 10 to 12 minutes until the bottoms are lightly browned. Quickly transfer to rack with wax paper under it.
- Put confectioner's sugar in a sifter and sprinkle over the cookies. Dip bottoms in confectioner's sugar. Place the cookies back on the rack and sift again.
- Cool.

NOTE: Instead of using the sifter, you can roll them in the sugar.

Romanesque Revival design by James Riely Gordon
Date – 1892

Bexar County's present-day courthouse is the direct heir of the oldest municipal government agency in Texas: the Cabildo. The Cabildo was the lowest administrative unit in the Spanish government that was set up in Spanish America in the sixteenth century.

San Antonio, Texas

Fayette County

La Grange, Texas

Fayette County

Cream Cheese and Poppy Seed Kolache Rolls

Submitted by Ed Janecka, Fayette County Judge

Ingredients:

SWEET YEAST DOUGH:
2 pkgs of active dry yeast
½ cup warm water
¾ cup lukewarm milk
1 cup margarine, melted
2 eggs, beaten
¼ cup sugar
1 tsp. salt
4½ cups flour

FILLING:
1 can poppy seed filling (enough for 2 rolls)
1 8oz. cream cheese
¼ to ½ cup sugar (as desired)
1 egg

This recipe will yield 4 rolls.

TEXAS JUDICIAL COOKBOOK

Preparation:

- Dissolve yeast in warm water. Combine with remaining ingredients in large bowl. Beat until smooth. About 1 minute.
- Cover with damp cloth. Place in refrigerator at least a couple hours or overnight.
- Divide roll in four balls. Roll out each ball of dough and fill with filling. Let rise for about 1 hour. Bake for about 20 minutes at 350°. Drizzle powdered sugar/milk mixture on top of roll while warm.

FILLING:

- Combine filling ingredients and mix well.
- Drop by spoonfuls onto rolled out dough.

Designed by James Riely Gordon
Date – 1891

Fayette County's county seat, La Grange, gets its name from the Marquis de Lafayette's estate in France and translates to "The Meadows."

The architect, Gordon, used a cruciform floor plan that drew air up from entrances and staircases through a central shaft of the courthouse and was surely appreciated during hot Texas summers.

La Grange, Texas

Lee County

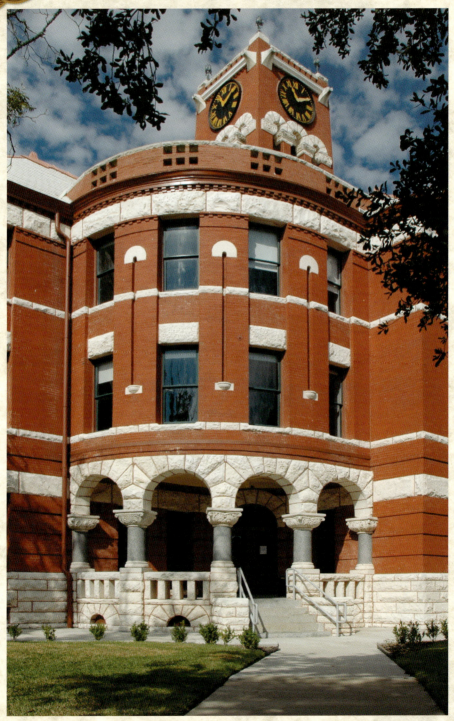

Giddings, Texas

Lee County

Chicken 'N Rice

Ingredients:

Chicken
1 stick margarine
1 can cream of mushroom soup
2 cups uncooked rice
1 can onion soup
2 cups chicken broth

*Submitted by Evan Gonzales,
Lee County Judge*

TEXAS JUDICIAL COOKBOOK

Preparation:

- Place all ingredients in a 9 x 13 inch pan.
- Place cut-up chicken, seasoned to your taste, on top. Cover.
- Cook 1 hour at 400°. Uncover and cook 30 minutes longer.

NOTE: *This dish along with a salad will make a wonderful meal.*

Designed by James Riely Gordon
Date – 1897

Lee County is named for Robert E. Lee, the commander-in-chief of the Confederate army.

Helpful Hint: To keep rice from clumping, add a few drops of lemon juice to it while simmering.

GIDDINGS, TEXAS

Concho County

Paint Rock, Texas

Concho County

Lasagna

Submitted by Allen Amos, Concho County Judge

"Before our wedding, Kathy served lasagna for my birthday. Thirty-eight years later, I'm the one who cooks it."

Ingredients:

1 lb. lean ground beef

1 to 2 cloves garlic

1 tablespoon basil

1 teaspoon salt

1 14½ oz. can Hunt's whole tomatoes, chopped, with juice

2 6 oz. cans Hunt's tomato paste

⅓ cup water

10 ozs. Lasagna noodles

24 ozs. Cottage cheese

½ cup grated Parmesan

2 tablespoons parsley flakes

2 beaten eggs

1 teaspoon salt (optional)

¼ teaspoon black pepper

12 ozs. Mozzarella sliced cheese

Texas Judicial Cookbook

Preparation:

- Brown meat slowly, spoon off excess fat.
- Add next six ingredients. Simmer uncovered on low heat for 30 minutes, stirring occasionally.
- Cook noodles as directed (easy on the salt).
- Combine remaining ingredients except mozzarella.
- In a 13 x 9 x 2 inch baking dish, layer half the noodles, half the cottage cheese mixture, half the mozzarella and half the meat sauce. Repeat layers.
- Bake at 375° for 30 minutes. Let stand 10 minutes before serving.

Second Empire design by F.E. Ruffini
Date – 1883

The county derives its name from the Concho (Spanish for "shell") River, whose name was based on the large number of mussels found in the area.

Paint Rock, Texas

Jasper County

Jasper, Texas

Jasper County

Hot Fried Cornbread

Submitted by Ted G. Walker, Jasper County, and wife Mary Lou

Ingredients:

1 cup yellow corn meal
1 cup white corn meal
¼ cup Bisquick Mix
½ teaspoon sugar
3 cups water with ½ t. salt added

Preparation:

- Mix dry ingredients, first 4.

- Bring to a boil the 3 cups of water with ½ teaspoon salt added. When water comes to a full boil, remove from heat and slowly add the dry ingredients to the boiling water, stirring constantly until well blended and thick.

- Spoon by tablespoon or make pone by hand.

- Drop into skillet of hot grease. Cook until golden brown.

NOTE: *Serve with pinto beans.*

Texas Judicial Cookbook

TEXAS JUDICIAL COOKBOOK

Broccoli Salad

Ingredients:

1 head broccoli cut into small pieces
1 lb. bacon fried crisp and crumbled
1 purple onion, diced
2 cups cheddar cheese

SAUCE:
1 cup mayo
½ cup sugar
2 tablespoons white vinegar
Dash of red pepper (Tabasco)
Dash of steak seasoning (Heinz 57)

*Submitted by
Ronald R. McBride,
Jasper County Sheriff*

Preparation:

- Toss broccoli, bacon, onion and cheese.
- Add sauce and let set several hours or overnight in refrigerator.

JASPER, TEXAS

Jasper County

Old Fashioned Southern Pecan Pie

Ingredients:

1 cup pecan halves
1 lb. box light brown sugar
¼ cup unsifted flour
½ teaspoon salt
½ cup milk
1½ teaspoons vanilla
3 eggs
½ cup melted butter (or margarine)

*Submitted by
Judge Joe Wilkinson,
Justice of the Peace, Precinct 4,
Jasper County*

TEXAS JUDICIAL COOKBOOK

PREPARATION:

- Heat oven to 325°.
- Place pecans in circular rings over bottom of uncooked pie shell.
- Blend sugar, flour and salt. Mix in the milk and vanilla. Beat in the eggs one at a time. Pour this over the pecans.
- Bake 1 hour and 15 minutes or until filling is puffy and crust is golden.
- Serve at room temperature.

NOTES: *Cut small pieces, this is a rich pie. If you enjoy pecan pie, like me, you'll love this one.*

*Renaissance Revival design by Eugene T. Heiner
Date – 1889*

The county was named for William Jasper, an American Revolutionary hero who was killed at the storming of Savannah in 1779.

Jasper County was originally part of the Spanish Atascosito District, which became Liberty District under Mexican rule.

JASPER, TEXAS

Throckmorton County

Throckmorton, Texas

Throckmorton County

Company Rice

Submitted by Mary Walraven, County and District Clerk, Throckmorton, Texas

INGREDIENTS:

1 cup long-grain rice
(not Minute Rice—long cooking)
1 can of Campbell's French Onion Soup
1 can of Campbell's Chicken Broth
2 cans whole water chestnuts, drained
2 bottles whole mushrooms, drained
1 stick of butter

PREPARATION:

- Place above ingredients in baking dish (2-qt. CorningWare). Add in order given. Do not stir.
- Place lid on baking dish and bake at 350° for 75 minutes, or until liquid is gone but rice is not dried out.

NOTES: *You may double the recipe.*

Good with roast, chicken, turkey, or pork.

TEXAS JUDICIAL COOKBOOK

Ruth's Salad

INGREDIENTS:

½ cup jicama
2 avocados
½ medium red onion
½ cup cilantro
1 large mango
Spring mix lettuce
Pine nuts

DRESSING:

⅓ cup cider vinegar
¼ cup olive oil
1 tablespoon honey
⅛ tablespoon cayenne pepper
Salt and pepper to taste

PREPARATION:

- Add all ingredients of salad together in large bowl.
- Mix all ingredients for dressing together and pour as desired over your salad.

NOTE: *A wonderful salad to have with friends.*

Italianate design
by Martin, Byrnes and Johnston
Date – 1890

The county was named for William E. Throckmorton, an early settler of north Texas and distinguished doctor of his day.

Throckmorton is the boyhood home of former Dallas Cowboy great, Bob Lilly, and sculptor, Joe Barrington.

THROCKMORTON, TEXAS

Glasscock County

Garden City, Texas

GLASSCOCK COUNTY

Apple Dumplings

*Submitted by
Wilburn E. Bednar,
Glasscock County Judge*

INGREDIENTS:

2 cans crescent rolls

2 Gala apples (peeled and cut in ⅛" slices)

1½ cups sugar

2 sticks Oleo

1 teaspoon cinnamon

1 12 oz. can of Mountain Dew

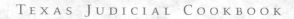

TEXAS JUDICIAL COOKBOOK

TEXAS JUDICIAL COOKBOOK

Preparation:

- Spray a 13 x 9 inch pan with Pam
- Wrap each slice in roll. Place in 2 rows, cut side down, in pan.
- In saucepan melt Oleo then add sugar, bring to boil.
- Pour the mixture in the middle of the pan of rolls.
- Pour 1 12 oz. can of Mountain Dew around the edge of the pan.
- Bake at 350° for 30 minutes.

Classical Revival design by Edward C. Hansford & Co. Date – 1909

The County Jail was Glasscock's courthouse before the 1909 one was built. Due to the county's small population, the jail has been vacant for years at a time.

The county was named for George W. Glasscock, a Texas Revolution officer and legislator.

 *Helpful Hint:* Best apples for pies and pastries: Cameo, Cortland, Golden Delicious, Granny Smith, Pink Lady, Rome.

GARDEN CITY, TEXAS

Wilson County

FLORESVILLE, TEXAS

Wilson County

Alene's Salad

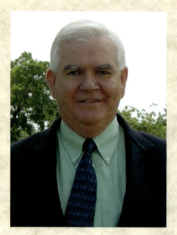

*Submitted by Marvin Quinney,
Wilson County Judge*

Ingredients:

1 cup chopped walnuts
1 bunch broccoli, chopped
1 head romaine lettuce
1 package Ramen noodles
4 green onions, chopped
4 tablespoons butter
Sweet and Sour dressing (below)

SWEET AND SOUR DRESSING:
1 cup vegetable oil
½ cup red wine vinegar
½ cup sugar
3 teaspoons Soy sauce
Salt and pepper to taste

Preparation:

- Brown nuts and noodles in butter. Cool on paper towel.
- Combine salad ingredients.

SWEET AND SOUR DRESSING:

- Blend together. Pour on salad.

Texas Judicial Cookbook

TEXAS JUDICIAL COOKBOOK

Fresh Apple Cake

Ingredients:

2 cups sugar
1 cup Wesson oil
¼ cup applesauce
3 eggs
1 teaspoon vanilla
½ cup hot water
3 cups flour
1 teaspoon baking soda
1 teaspoon baking powder
1 teaspoon salt
1 teaspoon cinnamon
4 apples
1 cup chopped pecans

Second Empire / Italianate design by Alfred Giles
Date – 1884

Preparation:

- Cream sugar, oil, applesauce, eggs and vanilla. Add hot tap water.
- Sift together flour, baking soda, baking powder, salt and cinnamon. Gradually add to creamed mixture.
- Stir in apples and nuts.
- Pour into a greased and floured Bundt pan. Bake at 350° for approximately one hour.

Each year there is a watermelon jubilee in the city of Stockdale in June and a peanut festival in Floresville in October.

Floresville, Texas

Barbara Bush

All-American Clam Chowder

"I love clam chowder soup and found this recipe to be very easy and delicious. I found it in Women's World many, many years ago and it's the only clam chowder soup I make."

Ingredients:

4 tablespoons butter or margarine
4 tablespoons flour
3 slices bacon, cut into 1-inch pieces
1 medium onion, finely chopped
1 can clams, drained, reserving juice
1 large potato, cubed
1 can cream of celery soup
1½ cups milk
1-dash pepper
oyster crackers, optional

Preparation:

- Cook bacon until crisp. Drain on paper towel. Sauté onion in same skillet as bacon until soft. Add clam juice and potatoes. Cover and cook over low heat for 15 minutes or until potatoes are tender. Melt butter in sauce pan. Add flour and mix together. Add milk and blend until smooth. Add clam juice and potatoes; cook and stir until thickened. Add soup, bacon, clams, and pepper; cook over low heat until heated through.

NOTE: *Serve with oyster crackers, if desired.*

The Texas Judicial Cookbook

Laura Bush

Carrot Muffins

Ingredients:

1 cup all-purpose flour
1 teaspoon baking soda
½ teaspoon ground cinnamon
2 eggs, room temperature
¾ cup canola or sunflower oil
1 teaspoon vanilla
1 cup sugar
1½ cups shredded carrot
½ cup coarsely chopped pecans

*Submitted by
First Lady Laura Bush,
Women's Health & Wellness,
The White House*

Preparation:

- Preheat oven to 350 degrees. Line 12 muffin molds with paper-cup liners. Combine flour, baking soda, and cinnamon in a medium bowl. Place the eggs, oil, vanilla, and sugar together in a mixing bowl. Whisk for about 5 minutes. Stir in flour mixture until combined. Stir in carrots and pecans. Fill cups ¾ full. Bake until a toothpick inserted into the center of a muffin comes out clean (approx. 18-20 minutes). Cool in pan for about 5 minutes and invert the muffins onto a rack.

NOTE: *Makes 12 muffins.*

Governor Rick Perry

Chuck Wagon Chili

Ingredients:

3 lbs. lean chili meat
1 15-oz. can tomato sauce
1 teaspoon red-hot sauce
3½ teaspoons chili powder
1½ teaspoons oregano
1 teaspoon cumin
1 teaspoon cayenne pepper
½ teaspoon salt
12 chili peppers
2 tablespoons flour (optional)
Water

Submitted by Governor Rick Perry, State of Texas, and wife, First Lady Anita Perry

Texas Judicial Cookbook

PREPARATION:

- Cut meat into 1-inch cubes. Place meat in large pot. Add tomato sauce and enough water to cover 1 inch above meat.

- Stir in red-hot sauce, chili powder, oregano, cumin, cayenne pepper, salt, and chili peppers. Simmer 1 hour 45 minutes. Skim off fat.

- If a thicker liquid is desired, combine 2 tablespoons flour and enough water to make a paste. Stir into chili. Simmer at least one minute longer.

- This is better if refrigerated overnight and heated before serving.

NOTES: *This recipe was so popular it was demonstrated for twelve years in a row on the Farm and Ranch News television program on KLTV in Tyler and KTRE in Lufkin.*

Makes 6-8 servings.

GOVERNOR RICK PERRY

Governor Rick Perry

Aunt Gene's Coconut Pie

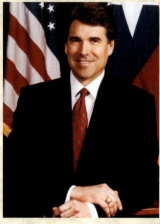

Submitted by Governor Rick Perry, State of Texas, and wife, First Lady Anita Perry

Ingredients:

½ cup sugar
¼ teaspoon salt
2 tablespoons cornstarch
¾ tablespoon flour
2¼ cups milk
2 lg. egg yolks
¾ tablespoon butter
1 teaspoon vanilla
¾ cup coconut
Baked pie shell
Meringue from two egg whites

TEXAS JUDICIAL COOKBOOK

PREPARATION:

- Mix together sugar, salt, cornstarch, and flour in saucepan. Gradually stir in milk. Cook over moderate heat, stirring constantly, until mixture thickens and boils. Boil for 1 minute. Remove from heat.

- Slowly stir half of the mixture into slightly beaten yolks. Blend egg mixture into saucepan. Boil for 1 minute, stirring constantly. Remove from heat.

- Blend in butter and vanilla. Cool mixture, stirring occasionally.

- Fold coconut into mixture. Pour pie filling into baked pie shell.

- Top with meringue. Bake at 450° for 5 minutes.

NOTE: *This recipe was Rick's favorite when he was growing up in the Haskell area, and it is still his favorite dessert.*

GOVERNOR RICK PERRY

JANET STAPLES

Mom's Chicken Pot Pie

*Submitted by Janet Staples,
Wife of Senator Todd Staples*

INGREDIENTS:

2 pie crusts

1 16 oz. can Veg-All mixed vegetables, drained

2 cans cream of potato soup

3 cups cooked, diced chicken

½ cup milk

½ teaspoons black pepper

PREPARATION:

- Line a deep dish or soufflé dish with one pie crust.

- Combine remaining 5 ingredients and spoon into crust.

- Top with remaining crust and crimp edges to seal. Slit top crust to allow steam to escape.

- Bake at 375° for 40 minutes. Cool for 10 minutes.

TEXAS JUDICIAL COOKBOOK

Mike Hamilton

Philadelphia Creamy Salsa Dip

Ingredients:

1 package (8 oz.) Philadelphia Fat-Free Cream Cheese

1 cup Taco Bell Home Originals Salsa and Variety

Preparation:

- Beat cream cheese until smooth.
- Add salsa; stir until well blended.
- Refrigerate or serve immediately.

NOTE: *Serve with assorted cut-up vegetables or tortilla chips.*

Submitted by Mike Hamilton, Texas State Representative, District 19

George Bush

President Bush's Favorite Brownies

Submitted by John Bauhs, Former White House Chef

Ingredients:

1¼ cups flour
¼ teaspoon baking soda
¼ teaspoon salt
½ cup (1 stick) butter
2 cups semisweet chocolate chips, divided
3 eggs
1½ teaspoons vanilla extract
1 cup sugar

Texas Judicial Cookbook

PREPARATION:

- Preheat oven to 350 degrees.
- In bowl, combine flour, baking soda, and salt.
- In a large saucepan, melt butter and 1 cup chocolate chips, stirring until smooth. (Or melt mixture in microwave for 1 minute at medium/50% power. Stir and microwave in 10-second increments if necessary. Do not overcook chocolate.)
- Add eggs and vanilla. Stir until well blended.
- Gently fold in flour mixture and sugar.
- Stir in remaining chocolate chips, and nuts if you please.
- Spread into greased 11 x 9 inch pan. Bake in preheated oven 15-20 minutes or until wooden toothpick inserted into center comes out almost clean.

NOTE: *Cool completely and cut into bars.*

This recipe is from John Bauhs, White House Chef when the first President Bush was in office. This recipe was given in an interview. According to Bauhs, President Bush likes his brownies to have a cake-like consistency and stand-out chocolate taste—but no nuts, please. To fulfill this request, half the chocolate chips are melted and mixed into the batter. The rest are stirred in whole.

GEORGE BUSH

George W. Bush

President Bush's Favorite Crab Cakes

Submitted by Sarah Bishop, Chef at the Governor's Mansion, Austin, Texas

Ingredients:

1 lb. jumbo lump blue crab meat
1 medium green bell pepper, finely chopped
2 ribs celery, finely chopped
1 egg
1 tablespoon mayonnaise
1 tablespoon lemon juice
Several dashes Tabasco sauce
1 pinch oregano
1 pinch basil
1 pinch salt and pepper
¾ cup breadcrumbs
Enough canola oil to coat the bottom of a heavy skillet about 1/8 inch.

Texas Judicial Cookbook

Preparation:

- Whisk egg, mayonnaise, lemon juice, and Tabasco sauce together.
- Fold crab meat, the egg-mayonnaise mix, and the chopped vegetables together.
- Add seasoning. Fold in breadcrumbs to bind.
- Form crab cakes by pressing firmly together in more breadcrumbs, coating thoroughly.
- Set on a sheet pan sprinkled with breadcrumbs. Allow to set in refrigerator.
- Panfry. Yields ten 3-ounce crab cakes.

NOTE: *Serve with lemon and tartar sauce.*

George W. Bush

Tom Craddick

Rum Cake

*Submitted by Tom Craddick,
Speaker of the House,
Texas House of Representatives,
and wife, Nadine*

Ingredients:

1 box Duncan Hines Yellow Cake Mix
1 large Jell-O Vanilla Instant Pudding
½ cup cooking oil
½ cup rum
½ cup water
4 eggs
½ cup chopped nuts

GLAZE:
1 cup sugar
1 cup butter
¼ cup water
2 oz. rum

Texas Judicial Cookbook

Preparation:

- Put all ingredients except nuts in large bowl. Mix well for 5-7 minutes.
- Grease bunt pan (I use Baker's Joy). Line bottom of pan with finely chopped nuts.
- Pour batter into prepared pan and bake at 350° for 1 hour. Leave in pan to cool.
- When almost cool, punch holes in top of cake with fork and pour hot glaze over cake.

GLAZE:

- Put all ingredients except rum in medium-size pot. Bring to boil. Boil for 1 minute. Remove from heat and add rum. Pour over cake. Leave cake in pan overnight.

NOTE: *Freezes Well.*

Tom Craddick

Leticia Van de Putte

Taco Pie

*Submitted by
Leticia Van de Putte,
Texas State Senator*

Ingredients:

1 frozen 9" deep dish pie crust
1½ cups shredded Monterey jack cheese
¼ lb cooked bacon, diced (save drippings)
1 medium onion, chopped
½ teaspoon ground cumin
¼ teaspoon oregano
¾ cup picante sauce
1 ripe avocado
Sour cream
Olive slices
Shredded lettuce & cilantro if desired

Texas Judicial Cookbook

PREPARATION:

- Bake crust according to directions.
- Put ½ cup cheese evenly over bottom of crust.
- Use 1 tablespoon of bacon drippings and add onion to skillet. Cook until tender.
- Add tomatoes, ½ cup picante sauce, cumin & oregano. Cook over high heat about 5 minutes.
- Spoon tomato mixture onto crust, top with bacon & rest of cheese. Bake at 375° until cheese is melted (about 5 minutes).
- Slice avocado into ½ inch thick slices. Arrange over pie and drizzle with rest of picante sauce. Garnish with sour cream, olives, lettuce and additional picante.

NOTE: *Makes 4 servings.*

LETICIA VAN DE PUTTE

Kay Bailey Hutchison

Cousin Susie's Perfect Fudge

Submitted by Kay Bailey Hutchison, United States Senator, Texas

Ingredients:

6 oz. package semi-sweet chocolate chips

6 oz. package butterscotch chips

(or I love it with a 12 oz. package milk chocolate chips)

1 can Eagle Brand milk

½ tsp. vanilla

1 cup chopped pecans (optional)

Preparation:

- Combine chips and milk and microwave for 2½ minutes. Stir and microwave for 2½ minutes more. Add vanilla and pecans. Pour into a greased glass pan and refrigerate.

Texas Judicial Cookbook

Texas Judicial Cookbook

Easy, Hearty Corn Chowder

Ingredients:

1 can creamed corn

1 can whole kernel corn

1 can cream of chicken soup

1 raw potato chopped in small pieces

¾ cup chopped celery

½ cup cooked and chopped bacon, sausage or ham

salt and pepper to taste

Preparation:

- Blend all ingredients and cook over low heat until potatoes and celery are done. Add water for desired thickness.

Kay Bailey Hutchison

Bibliography

Thank you to these sites for information on counties, courthouses and food tips.

"11 Most Endangered Places: Historic Courthouses of Texas." National Trust for Historic Preservation. Dec 2005. http://www.nationaltrust.org/11Most/list.asp?i=10

CDKitchen Cooking Tips
http://www.cdkitchen.com/features/tips.php

County of Bandera, Texas
www.banderacounty.org

County of Bell, Texas
www.bellcountytx.com/history.htm

Dictionary.com
http://dictionary.reference.com

Ellis County Museum
www.rootsweb.com/~txecm/

Jefferson County, Texas
www.co.jefferson.tx.us/Historical_Commission/hist.htm

LifeTips
http://cooking.lifetips.com/cat/7746/cooking-tips/index.html

Ludwig, Michael. "Secrets to Cooking TexMex." TEXMEX.net. 2005.
www.texmex.net/Rotel/main.htm

Oaks, F. Lawrence. "Texas Historic Courthouse Preservation Program." Texas Historical Commission. Plan filed on 5 Nov 2002. http://texinfo.library.unt.edu/texasregister/html/2002/nov-22/PROPOSED/13.CULTURAL%20RESOURCES.html

TexasEscapes
www.texasescapes.com/Texas_architecture/TexasCourthouses.htm

"Texas Historic Courthouse Preservation Program, Austin, Texas, Receives a National Trust National Preservation Honor Award." National Trust for Historic Preservation. 30 Sept 2004.
http://www.nationaltrust.org/news/docs/20040930_awards_courthouse.html

The Texas State Historical Association
www.tsha.utexas.edu

The TXGenWeb Project
www.rootsweb.com/~txjasper/
www.rootsweb.com/~txgrimes/

Touchstone Bernays, Attorneys at Law
www.touchstonelaw.com/courthouses.htm

Throckmorton County Chamber of Commerce
www.throckmortontx.com/Chamber%20of%20Commerce.htm

United States Department of Agriculture: Food Safety and Inspection Service.
http://www.fsis.usda.gov/Fact_Sheets/Chicken_Food_Safety_Focus/index.asp

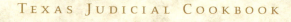

TEXAS JUDICIAL COOKBOOK